Concentration and Meditation

BY

SWAMI PARAMANANDA

Sri Ramakrishna Math,
Mylapore, Msdras-4.

Published by :
© The President,
Sri Ramakrishna Math,
Mylapore, Madras 600 004.

Ninth Impression
IX-5M 3C-1-97
ISBN 81-7120-266-7

Printed in India at
Sri Ramakrishna Math Printing Press,
Mylapore, Madras 600 004.

CONTENTS

I.
CONCENTRATION

If, therefore, thine eye be single, thy whole body shall be full of light. —*Jesus the Christ.*

If you are perfectly pure and practise faithfully, your mind can finally be made a searchlight of infinite power. There is no limit to its scope. —*Swami Vivekananda.*

The well-resolved mind is single and one-pointed, but the purposes of the irresolute mind are many-branched and endless. —*Bhagavad-Gita.*

Keep your body under proper control, your gaze concentrated upon One, and the peace of God will descend upon you. —*Chuang-Tzu.*

THE faculty of concentration is innate in every living creature. Among animals, we see a lion or tiger gathering his strength by a moment of absolute stillness before he springs upon his prey. That automatic, instinctive power we all possess, but with the majority it is not cultivated, and we never shall have the full use of it until we gain conscious command over our mental and spiritual forces.

Focused mind like a searchlight. We know that when light is dissipated we cannot see well, but when the scattered rays are brought together by the help of a shade or reflector, then everything grows distinct. In the same way, when our scattered mental forces are gathered up and focused, the mind becomes like a bright searchlight, by means of which man is able to investigate the latent powers of his own innermost being. As he grows more aware of these hidden forces and learns to use them, he becomes ever more and more proficient in life.

The reason for defeat. We never wish to be defeated and yet how often our strength of mind or our physical capacity proves inadequate. It is because we have not the full and conscious possession of our whole being.

Value of one-pointedness. Man can achieve very little unless he has free use of his hands and feet, free use of his eyes and ears, free use of his muscles and above all free use of his mind and intelligence. But how many of us have the free use of all these? When we would employ them we find them hopelessly scattered, and rebellious to our will. The cause of this does not lie in any inherent lack of power, but in our inability to co-ordinate, and in our lack of definite one-pointed purpose. We miss the mark because we do not set our aim properly.

Arjuna's victory.

Once, in ancient India, there was a tournament held to test marksmanship in archery. A wooden fish was set up on a high pole and the eye of the fish was the target. One by one, many valiant princes came and tried their skill, but in vain. Before each one shot his arrow the teacher asked him what he saw and invariably all replied that they saw a fish on a pole at a great height, with head, eyes, etc.; but Arjuna, the great hero, as he took his aim, said: "I see only the eye of the fish," and he it was who succeeded in hitting the mark.

Forger of swords. A similar incident is given by the Chinese sage, Chuang-Tzu: "The man who forged swords for the Minister of War was eighty years of age. Yet he never made the slightest slip in his work. The Minister of War said to him: 'Is it your skill, sir, or have you any method?'

" 'It is concentration,' replied the man. 'When twenty years old, I took to forging swords. I cared for nothing else. If a thing was not a sword, I did not notice it. I availed myself of whatever energy I did not use in other directions in order to secure greater efficiency in the direction required.' "

Concentration means wholeness. Concentration means wholeness, unity, equilibrium. All our members and faculties must be unified. They must work in harmony, in tranquility and balance. Balance is needed everywhere in life. A man may be over-active or he may be idle; both extremes indicate an absence of poise, of self-adjustment.

Moderation essential. Sri Krishna declares in the Gita: "O Arjuna, the practice of Yoga is not for him who eats too much or who does not eat at all, nor for him who sleeps too much or who keeps awake in excess. He who is moderate in eating and recreation, moderate in his efforts in work, moderate in sleep and wakefulness, his practice of Yoga destroys all misery."

Lack of balance means lack of strength. What does this signify? That he who goes to extremes is a slave of impulse—he is not the master. He lacks balance. Lack of balance means lack of strength and without strength no great work can be accomplished. If, on the contrary, we practise moderation or equilibrium, even in our most ordinary daily tasks, we shall see how steady will be our gain in concentration.

Tapas or self-discipline. The practice of moderation necessitates a certain amount of self-discipline. The Hindus call this *Tapas,* which means literally "fire" or "heat," and they believe that unless this fire of self-discipline is lighted, in order to burn to ashes all the impurities and limitations of our system, spiritual illumination will be impossible. But here, too, extremes must be avoided.

Over-strain harmful. Often people through misunderstanding or over-enthusiasm torture and strain themselves in the hope of advancing more rapidly, but they defeat their own ends.

Purpose of discipline. Excessive penance or mortification is as harmful as self-indulgence. The purpose of all discipline is to make our constitution more enduring, more adaptable and more responsive. Body and mind must be made wholly obedient to the will and independent of outer circumstances.

Methods of discipline. The person who is a slave to physical comforts should gradually eliminate all that is superfluous and train himself to be content with the bare necessities. Any one who finds it difficult to overcome physical lethargy and rise early in the morning should drag himself out of bed by sheer force of will. One who is inclined to over-eating should by degrees reduce the quantity of his food. A person who has the habit of talking unnecessarily should practise stillness by persistent control of all useless motions. Such practices not only increase our power of concentration and meditation, but do much to improve our bodily health and make us happier in every way. Also as we learn to meditate, our outer being falls into rhythm.

Meditation inseparable from concentration. Meditation is inseparable from concentration. When the mind has gained its full strength through singleness, it naturally becomes meditative.

Mind like a lake. Often the mind is compared to a lake. If the surface is absolutely smooth—not a ripple—then we can see clearly what lies beneath. Similarly when the mind becomes calm, when the wind of uncontrolled desire does not constantly create ripples over the surface of it, then the image of our true nature is not broken and we obtain a perfect reflection of what we are in reality and what our relation is with the Supreme Intelligence. As long as the mind is agitated, so long our vision can never be unerring.

Happiness comes from within. Constantly we are hoping that some one else may give us knowledge and happiness, but that is not possible. These come only from within.

Need for spiritual activity. What we need is to be active spiritually. As we go on living our outer life, we must devote some time each day to making our mind introspective, that we may develop our subtler powers of perception.

Mind a scientific instrument. In all investigations certain instruments are necessary, as we see scientists inventing finer and finer instruments for their investigations. Also for spiritual observation we need a form of mind which can discern the subtler things, imperceptible to our ordinary sense-faculties. The concentrated mind is such an instrument and the only one fitted for higher research.

Why the mind is weak. Our mind at present is weak only because it is disorganized and divided. When through determined and steadfast practice, we gather up our mental forces and focus them, the hidden powers of the universe will be revealed to us.

Lower forms of concentration. We must not, however, remain content with the lower forms of concentration. These may bring us physical health, prosperity or success, but even after we have acquired all that outer life can give, we shall find that one part of our being still remains unsatisfied. Never will it be satisfied until we awaken to the Reality within us and begin to work for our higher development. Nor should such work be regarded as selfish, because all human beings are bound together, therefore as we unfold our own spiritual nature, we cannot fail to benefit others.

One life through all. The same life runs through and through all creation; and only he who can seize hold of that subtle spiritual essence hidden in the heart will know how to solve the riddle of this human existence. Such a man alone lives happily and fearlessly.

Why we fear. Now, we are fearful because so many things are hidden from us: we fear the future because we do not know what the future may bring; we fear death because we are not sure what may come after. For this reason, we must learn to focus the mind and turn it within; by its brilliant light we shall understand all things and attain the vision of Truth which does away with fear. The purpose of meditation—of all our spiritual practice—is to gain that vision. Nor must we stop until we have seen by direct perception our true Self and our relation with the Supreme. As we concentrate on that which is All-Light, the darkness of mind and body will vanish as night before the dawn.

Mind but a reflex.

There is only one Power, one Intelligence, one Mind, which is God, and our mind is nothing but a reflex of That. So long as it works apart from that universal Mind, it remains unintelligent, ignorant, powerless; but when it becomes united with It through one-pointed striving, it attains a state of complete illumination: "After having attained which, no other gain seems greater; being established wherein, man is not overwhelmed even by great sorrow."

II.
KEY TO CONCENTRATION

All the genius I have lies just in this: When I have a subject in hand, I study it profoundly. Day and night it is before me. I explore it in all its bearings; my mind becomes pervaded with it. Then the effort which I make the people are pleased to call the fruit of genius. It is the fruit of labor and thought. —*Alexander Hamilton.*

I go at what I am about as if there were nothing else in the world for the time being. That's the secret of all hard-working men. —*Charles Kingsley.*

Thought is best when the mind is gathered into herself and is aspiring after true being. —*Socrates.*

For it is not possible to see Him or be in harmony with Him while one is occupied with anything else. The soul must remove from itself everything, that it may receive the One alone, as the One is alone. —*Plotinus.*

THE practice of holding to one subject is the real key to concentration. Patanjali, the father of the Yoga System, advocates this, and wherever we find its practical evidence, we find that this method has been applied. It is the one eternal principle in mental control.

Speed and efficiency.

The fact is, we cannot do more than one thing at a time and do it well. But if we concentrate on that one thing wholly, we succeed not only in doing it well, we do it much more quickly, thus we save our time and energy for the next task which lies before us. This is very essential in every phase and department of human interest.

Value of change. Do not imagine, however, that the practice of concentration implies that you must dwell upon just one thing and do nothing else, even when you are tired and bored and discouraged through repeated unsuccessful efforts. A change of physical and mental occupation sometimes is necessary and beneficial. You will go back to your task with fresh interest and renewed vigor, and naturally you will be able to make greater progress.

The views of a noted educator. "Physical diversion or a change in the form of our mental activity," says Dr. Frederick Robinson, noted educator, "may pave the way for a solution of some long-pondered problem. As students, many of us have had this experience. After working hard at night on some particular problem, we have solved it with ease the next morning. Such work, accomplished by the mind without our consciously directing its activities, would appear to be the very opposite of concentration. But remember that without the intense, concentrated effort that went before, such flashes of insight are rare.

Time versus concentration. "The great difference between those who achieve and those who fail consists not so much in the amount of time devoted to work by each, but in the degree to which he intelligently applies his powers, mental and physical, to one purpose."

Discouragement an obstacle. Do not be discouraged ever, as you struggle along the way. It is the greatest possible detriment to your progress, the worst obstacle you can create to block your path. One who is discouraged denies his true Self, his inherent, divine being.

Concentration a definite cure. Concentration is a definite cure for all manner of mental disturbances. As we focus our mind on a constructive principle, uneasiness, restlessness, worry, the attitude of self-depreciation,—all these ailments are crowded out of our system.

Co-ordination of the whole man. Concentration does not depend upon how much time we spend, but on how well we hold ourselves together. As we are able to co-ordinate our body, our mind, and all our scattered forces and succeed in making them as one, we realize in full measure our innate efficiency.

Right choice of ideal. The mind possesses an enormous quantity of material for thought, and often an unproductive mind is more filled with ideas than is one engaged in some specific line of action. The secret of success lies not so much in abundance of thought as in our ability to follow one well-chosen subject to the exclusion of all others.

This subject we ourselves must choose. The right choice of subject helps immensely. It builds up our life and aids us in climbing the ladder of true success, step by step.

An excellent slogan.

There is nothing insignificant anywhere. This is an excellent slogan to carry in the mind. Give your attention to the smallest of tasks; do everything with feeling, with true devotion—it is the best way to build up the habit of concentration. A small task well done will give you the power to do a bigger one better.

Key to true knowledge.

The practice of concentration, even in little things, helps us to organize the chaotic elements in our body, and as the practice becomes a habit, gradually we establish ourselves in a state of physical health and mental alertness which finds its expression in dynamic, exhilarating thoughts, buoyant optimism, and high inspiration. Also we gain in the ability to pursue ever higher thoughts and ideals. Thus this practice proves to be the only key to true knowledge.

Wrong concentration. Wrong concentration, as well, may bring us moments of satisfaction through the gratification of our lower desires, but in the end it leads to the demoralization of our entire system; for wrong-doing can never earn for us the right to happiness.

What wrong concentration means. By wrong concentration I mean the deliberate focusing of mental energy in order to harm some one. Although temporarily a person may be successful in his ill use of this great power, eventually it cannot fail to react upon him. "He whose mind is not tranquil can know neither peace nor happiness."

Unconscious concentration. Often, quite unconsciously, we concentrate on something that is detrimental. Violent emotion—anger or hatred for instance—will focus the mind in a manner that is hurtful to ourselves and others.

Also the mind can be focused by worry. This cannot be called concentration, yet it does cause the mind to go round and round a subject in a negative and destructive way.

Wrong methods.

It may sound strange and incongruous to connect concentration with anything negative. Usually we understand by concentration something that is strong, potent, vibrant. If, however, our mind forms a habit of dwelling upon that which is morbid or of no consequence—as, for instance, when an individual indulges in thoughts of brooding or self-pity—gradually we develop these wrong and negative methods.

Negative concentration.

Negative concentration, instead of giving us any benefit, weakens us and often causes an acute form of melancholia. The cure for all these mental disorders is positive concentration. In fact, real concentration always should be understood in terms of definiteness and positiveness.

Concentration an art. Every human being has the faculty of concentration, but every human being has not acquired the power of directing the mind toward that which is creative, constructive and helpful. It is an art which we have to learn by degrees.

The flexible mind. One of the immediate results we obtain through the practice of right concentration is that our mind grows strong and flexible. It adapts itself with great ease to whatever may be placed before it, even something that is out of its accustomed line.

Value of relaxation. The most effectual mentality does not express itself through tenseness; yet the average individual, in the act of accomplishing something, makes himself so tense and rigid that he comes almost to the breaking-point. This is just the opposite of the true method. Right concentration makes us calm and collected and we emanate serene strength. Also our thoughts function most freely and can be focused with greater effectiveness when the mind and body are relaxed and tranquil.

Serene-mindedness. Never be in a hurry: learn to be poised and thoughtful. The man who has gained even in small measure the power of concentration moves quietly with a sense of leisure, as if there were nothing else in the entire universe but that one task laid before him.

From atom to Infinite. When the mind is concentrated on any subject which stands for vitality, energy, action or spiritual poise, it connects us, as it were, with the reservoir of these wonderful spiritual qualities. By concentration we can unite ourselves with all things, from the minutest to the biggest, from the lowest to the highest. As it is truly said by the Yogi, "Through mastery of concentration one gains access everywhere, from the atom to the Infinite."

III.
POWER OF CONCENTRATION

Concentration is the secret of strength in war, in trade; in short, in all the management of human affairs.

—Emerson.

Thou hast the power of taking thought, of seeing it and grasping it in thy own "hands" and gazing face to face upon God's image. ***—Hermes Trismegistus.***

The man who has daily inured himself to habits of concentrated attention, energetic volition and self-denial in unnecessary things will stand like a tower when everything rocks around him and when his softer fellow-mortals are winnowed like chaff in the blast. ***—William James.***

By concentration one obtains stability of the mind.

—Jain Teaching.

Meditate on the mind! He who meditates on the mind is, as it were, lord and master as far as the mind reaches.

—Chandogya Upanishad.

CONCENTRATION gives power. We all understand this to a certain extent, but largely as an intellectual concept. Today many believe that whatever they desire they can obtain by concentrating upon it. That is a cheap form of psychological practice. Merely gaining that upon which we have set our heart does not make for true success, otherwise a greater number of people would be successful. The thief concentrates upon his victim and steals his purse, yet we do not envy him his action. Temporarily he may seem to gain his end—and that has great popular appeal—but the fabric of his character is weakened.

Wrong choice and reaction. Whatever a man wants he can obtain. By degrees we accomplish our end. That is why we must purify our desires that we may not want the wrong thing, because whenever we make a wrong choice and work for it there is always the reaction. Moreover, after we have achieved our aim, we may find that we no longer desire it.

Concentration means self-control. Concentration implies great self-control. One who has no control over himself, who is easily upset, made angry or revengeful, such a one lacks true concentration, although he may long to have the power which it gives. Owing to his weakness, he cannot have it. True concentration means strength—strength of mind, strength of character—and cannot be used for destructive purposes or to satisfy petty personal desires.

Source of strength. Our desire should be for that which makes us strong—strong to meet unexpected shocks—depression, chaos, uncertainty—and this strength does not depend on material resources but on poise and mental calibre.

The main idea. The main idea of concentration is to make of ourselves a channel, so clear, so direct, so unbiased, that through our instrumentality the power of Divinity can flow and accomplish Its great end. Keep this always in mind.

Physical and mental habits. Concentration means effort. It means overcoming physical and mental habits. People by means of their mental strength can overcome physical habits, but mental habits are more difficult to control.

The mind always can help us overcome physical tendencies. In fact, if the mind is strong enough and the desire sufficiently one-pointed, even habits of long duration, such as drinking and the drug habit, can be conquered through the mind. When we come to mental habits, however, if we have not a good, collected and flexible mind, we are confronted with a far greater difficulty.

Mental standards. It is not that there is a lack of mental standards, but mental standards are not enough. If they were, Christ, Buddha and other Master-Spirits would have changed the world. Great Ones give, but man cannot always receive. He has the power to make his own interpretation. He can see everything clear and shining or through the eyes of distortion. When the sun is visible, he can make himself believe it is a mirage. When the possibility of good fortune arises, he can persuade himself that it is only a trap. Mind alone creates such conditions, therefore mind itself must be its own subject of concentration.

Words of Sri Krishna. In the Bhagavad-Gita, Sri Krishna gives a wonderful picture of the concentrated mind: "As a lamp placed in a windless spot does not flicker, the same simile is used to define a Yogi of subdued mind practising union with the Self."

Again, Sri Krishna tells us: "When the mind is completely subdued by the practice of Yoga, and has attained serenity, in that state, seeing Self by the self, he is satisfied in the Self alone."

Slavery to externals. The average person craves diverse outside interests. In fact, the less a man is nourished inwardly, the more does he want outer contact, companionship and diversion. Not only does he want them, he must have them. It becomes a sort of slavery, like the habit for narcotics. It can, however, be cured by a simple turn of mind.

Inner unfoldment. The moment the mind becomes truly focused, we seem to enter a new province. Something is unfolded from within, and, like a man who has discovered a gold mine, we can think of nothing else, we can speak of nothing else. "Seeing Self by the self, we are satisfied in the Self alone."

Realization a definite experience. The idea of Self-realization must not be taken in any vague sense. It is a definite experience. This blundering, frail and faltering person that we call our self is aware all at once of an unlimited source of supply. Here we find the real source of all genius. A musician often becomes so absorbed in his work of creation that he forgets his food and drink and bodily needs. The same way it is with the artist, the inventor, with any one whose mind is focused on a single goal.

The master-touch. A tremendous force would be conserved in and for society through the right use of concentration. The one who possesses this gift is successful everywhere. When he does a bit of so-called menial service, it is with a master-touch. If he is given something fine and subtle to do, that too is skilfully performed, because the same mind lends its aid.

Concentration of body and mind. Concentration is a faculty of both body and soul. There is physical concentration and there is mental concentration. Physical concentration means gathering together every ounce of bodily strength and directing it one-pointedly. Mental concentration is far more difficult, but it gives unlimited power to the mind.

Haunting memories. The true form of concentration requires a dynamic attitude. Often when the mind is harassed by the memory of painful experiences, disappointments, sad associations, we try to make our escape by means of a negative process—we strive to empty the mind, to cease thinking, in the hope that thus we shall find peace. Occasionally a little relaxation comes this way, but real peace is never gained through negation: it is due to mental control.

Sentinel thought. The thing is, we should not strive to empty the mind of thought; rather we should fill it so completely with one vital, vibrant, constructive thought, that no other thought can find entrance.

Gradual attainment. We cannot achieve all at once any great ideal. Our present stature, position, tendencies have to be readjusted and the process of readjustment takes a shorter or longer time according to the *earnestness* and *persistence* of the efforts we make. I mean this in every sense of the word.

Mental spendthrift. In moments of great exuberance and upliftment, your mind, your senses and all your faculties seem to blend. For the time, you find no difficulty in concentrating your mind upon any subject.

Then you grow careless. You settle down and live on your past experience and the success that went with it, feeling that the merit you attained at that period will carry you without any further effort on your part. You become like an improvident person trying to live on his inheritance. Although he may have had a fortune to begin with, it soon dwindles to nothing.

Tuning our instrument. The practice of concentration is very much like keeping a musical instrument in tune. A musician who loves his instrument does not neglect it, even when he is not going to play before the public. We may not need all our powers of concentration to do what is immediately before us, but we never know when a crisis may arise. That is why we cannot afford to neglect the mind.

Illumined mind a vessel of gold. Sri Ramakrishna, the great Master of modern India, gives in his teachings a wonderful, a very vivid illustration in regard to this subject of mental practice. Every man, he says, should make a legitimate effort to keep his mind in a good, clean, concentrated condition, otherwise it grows unsightly—like a metal vessel which becomes tarnished if it is not polished every day. A golden vessel, however, does not have to be polished so frequently. So with our mind. Once it touches the Supreme, it becomes like the vessel of gold—it retains its sunlike splendor, its shining quality, even when it is not given any special care. When mind makes its point of contact with the central Source of life and power, all our troubles end.

Armor of prayer. These principles you must learn to apply. When conditions become harrowing and you feel powerless, then hold fast. Do not permit things to crowd in on your mind. Create a barrier—a wall. Take a thought or a little prayer or a poem—anything of spiritual significance—

and form an armor about you. Instead of letting the mind revolve round and round your aches and pains and sicknesses, take a firm stand and fasten your thought to the Infinite. This practice will bring wholeness and healing.

Lotus of the heart. From the very outset, banish all impatience. Impatience only makes your road harder. Be steadfast, resolute and enduring. No matter how many times you may seem to fail, bring the mind back and focus it on the Ideal, focus it on the lotus of the heart, full of light, full of purity, untainted by sin and sorrow. In this way, and in this way alone, you will know and realize and enter into the meaning of that profound truth: "As a man thinketh in his heart, so is he!" So shall he make himself to be.

IV.
MEDITATION

"To him who is perfect in meditation salvation is very near," is an old saying. Do you know when a man becomes perfect in meditation? When as soon as he sits down to meditate he becomes surrounded with divine atmosphere and his soul communes with God. —*Sri Ramakrishna.*

Change thy thought from the world and cast it wholly on Him and He shall nourish thee. —*Richard Rolle.*

Perfection in meditation comes from persevering devotion to the Supreme. —*Patanjali.*

WHEN the mind is poised and well concentrated, the supreme Self of man becomes visible. At other times we do not see the real man and the apparent man thinks himself all in all. The Seer or higher Self is there, but we are not conscious of it. When, however, the mind becomes clarified, the Self appears in Its true state and we do not have to make any effort to perceive It.

Disturbing mental waves.

So long as there is any disturbance in our mind, we cannot see things as they are in truth; we cannot obtain the vision of our true Self. All these waves—selfishness, ambition, desire—must subside, and the mind be made one-pointed. When a man attains this, he beholds the Self. At other times he identifies himself with some passing mental adjunct like anger or jealousy or fear.

Why we suffer. If we analyze, we shall see that when any one speaks harshly to us, the word is first outside us, then it enters into us, and we grow angry. At first anger and we are separate, then become one: we identify ourselves with anger and we suffer. We suffer because we come in contact with so many things that are not in harmony with our real nature.

Discrimination of the Yogi or wise man. Yoga means disuniting the mind from all disturbing influences. The truly wise man, or the Yogi, does not identify himself with these states or modifications of mind and body. He does everything like other people—eats, sleeps, works—but his actions differ from others owing to the fact that he knows the distinction between the true Self and the ego. He realizes that all these outer things exist only because the Self is behind them, and being conscious of That alone, he goes through the various experiences of life without being affected by them.

Wrong identification. As long as we identify ourselves with passing conditions, we suffer; but when we cease to identify ourselves with these conditions, then we never really suffer.

Mental modifications. At present our mind is going in many directions. We must turn it and direct it toward a fixed goal. We must train it to differentiate itself from its modifications. Now, if something agreeable happens, we feel pleasure; if something disagreeable comes, we feel pain. But this pleasure and pain are only momentary. When in both we can keep the mind steady, we gain lasting concentration.

The three Qualities or Gunas. The mind falls naturally into three general states: the dull state; the over-active or scattered state; and the calm, centred state. These correspond to the three *Gunas* or Qualities of matter, called in Sanskrit, *Tamas, Rajas,* and *Sattwa.* These Qualities are innate in every living thing and manifest in the human mind as the subconscious, conscious and superconscious.

First Quality. The first Quality is that of darkness, inertia, heaviness—the brute state. The mind, in this state, is dull, slothful, and does not wish to exert itself in any direction. Not that it lacks in desire—it is full of desires—but it is overpowered by a heaviness which keeps it from making the necessary effort to satisfy them. Also it lacks in power to differentiate between right and wrong and is easily carried away by lower animal instincts.

Second Quality.

The second Quality—that of excessive ambition, egotism, arrogance and discontent—causes the mind to be in the state known as scattered (*Vikshipta*). When this Quality is in ascendency, a man is consumed by feverish unrest and an irresistible longing to multiply possessions and to entangle himself more and more in external undertakings. His energies are dissipated and often wasted; his thoughts move hither and thither without any sense of responsibility. No matter how great his achievements, he is never satisfied, for the flame of his desire mounts with each new gratification, as a fire fed by fresh fuel. So long as the mind is thus wandering and scattered, we can never accomplish anything—so the Yogis say—nor can we hope to find peace. Yet remember, this is only a passing state. The mind is not that, it merely lacks the power to separate itself from conditions which have covered it.

Third Quality. With the third Quality—*Sattwa*—the mind grows collected, serene, and illumined. This is the concentrated state (*Ekagra*), through which we become one with the object of our worship. It is the fitting state for spiritual attainment, the final aim of Yoga, for it leads to union or communion with God.

Attainment a natural process. In order to reach this high point of attainment, we must go through a natural process: the condition of dullness or inertia must be conquered by stimulating all the physical and mental activities. Then these activities must be regulated and directed until they are focused. The subconscious must be brought into complete subjection to the conscious and the conscious must be expanded into the higher state of superconsciousness, or *Samadhi*.

Samadhi or superconsciousness. When the mind, in *Samadhi*, becomes fixed on the Supreme Being, when through meditation we are united with that Power, then we have fulness of vision.

Way of superconsciousness. The first practice in acquiring the concentrated state is to attach the mind to one point, the object of our search. When we have accomplished this, if we can then hold our thought there unwaveringly—without any modification—for twelve seconds, it will constitute a *Dhyana* or meditation; twelve of these will give *Samadhi*. That is, twelve such meditations, in unbroken sequence, will bring superconscious vision.

Unity of thought. So long as there is a sense of division in the mind and we are struggling to concentrate, there cannot be meditation; for meditation means a state of mental collectiveness where the thought flows like oil poured from one vessel to another.

Firmness and perseverance. At present our mind is in a constant struggle. We have indulged it all our life, so now when we try to make it obey, it rebels. Therefore our practice must be carried on with firmness and determination. When the mind finds that we will not obey it, then it will obey us. The same is true of the body, for that which makes both body and mind act is Spirit.

The driver and the chariot. The body is like a chariot, the senses are like horses, and mind is like the reins. Only by holding firmly to the reins can we keep control. If we do not, these sense-horses will drag us away.

How the mind becomes pure. We must strive to fix our mind on our Ideal. Many think it best to fix it on some simple, outer object first; but this mechanical practice is a very low form of concentration and gives us only limited results. It is better to hold the mind upon inner spiritual objects,—on infinite strength, infinite wisdom, infinite love or purity, on the effulgent flame of life seated in the heart, on anything through which the current of divine life is running. While these pure thoughts fill our consciousness, there will be no room for impurity, and if we continue this practice, little by little the mind will become pure. By meditating in this way, if only for three or four minutes, we shall be like different beings: we shall be so filled with peace, power and light.

Harmony with our ideal. In order to accomplish this, however, we must bring our mind into perfect harmony with our Ideal. Then alone we shall be happy, for all unhappiness is caused by friction or duality.

The barrier of impurity. When we meditate on purity, if unkind thoughts arise within us, how can we hold the thought of purity? We may be surrounded with the most beautiful flowers, we may have holy pictures and burn incense, but if our mind is impure, that is, not one-pointed—fixed on the Ideal—we shall never know holiness.

The pure mind invulnerable

Any outside condition can be overcome through the power of concentration, because the mind when focused becomes strong and is able to shut out whatever disturbs it. Nothing can overwhelm us when our mind rests firmly in holiness, purity and love.

Scattered mind like a thread.

The scattered mind is like a single thread: it can easily be broken; but the concentrated mind is like many pieces of thread twisted together: it is difficult to break. Therefore we must govern our thoughts and hold them steadily on the object of our concentration.

Overcoming the external.

If the mind is concentrated, we do not hear anything, we do not see anything—all our senses are in abeyance. External sounds, external vision, all external sense perceptions can be overcome by concentration.

Highest form of meditation

Intensity of concentration leads to meditation. But meditation is not easy. It means feeling the presence of God within. The highest form of meditation is to fix the mind on the Real, the Unchangeable.

Beauty beyond the object.

An artist through concentration on some object in nature succeeds in painting a beautiful picture. If, however, he carries his thought on to the idea of beauty beyond the object, then he may attain meditation.

Artists of the Far East.

Count Hermann Keyserling in his "Travel Diary of a Philosopher," refers to the meditative powers of the great artists of China and Japan.

Yoga the path to art.

He shows that not only were they all Yogis, but they saw in Yoga the only true path to art. It was not that technical training was ignored or neglected. During their student years, he assures us, they drew after nature with great persistence till they became masters of line and color; but they looked on this as only a preliminary. Their real problem was through contemplation to become so absorbed in the spirit of their subject, no matter what it might be—a mountain, a tree in winter or a human face—that they could recreate it from within, confident that the outer form would be in rhythm.

The Chinese conception.

In illustration of this, he tells us of Li Lung-Mien, a master of the Sung Dynasty, whose working hours were largely spent in meditation on the slopes of hills or beside streams. Also he cites Wu Tao-tse who when commanded by the emperor to paint a certain landscape, returned after a long absence without even a single sketch. In answer to the emperor's angry questionings, he quietly replied: "I have brought it all back in my heart!" Kuo Hsi, in his famous treatise on landscape painting, writes: "An artist must, above everything else, enter into spiritual harmony with the hills and rivers he desires to paint."

Meditation conquers space. Ordinarily we can see only that person who is near; we cannot see one who is far. Meditation is the power which enables us to see and draw near to a person thousands of miles away. Sometimes this meditation comes in sleep, and sometimes as a pure vision, by meditating on which we may acquire wisdom.

Piercing the veil. Wisdom means steadiness, balance. Lack of balance creates a veil and clouds our vision. The moment we concentrate our mind, however, we pierce through the veil and at once see clearly. When a man gains a steady mind, he can penetrate any veil, external or internal, as light penetrates darkness.

Meditation adds to sensitiveness. Through concentration we develop extraordinary sense perceptions. We sense things which other people cannot. If some one holds unkind thoughts, we perceive it, and if any one holds a loving thought, we feel that at once also. We dwell closer to God and thus can feel more keenly what others feel—we have a greater sympathy. But this does not mean that we suffer more. That one alone really suffers who lives in ignorance and selfishness.

Teaching of Patanjali. Patanjali says in his Yoga aphorisms, "Whatever our mind constantly dwells upon, that we become." Our thought forms a point of connection between us and the object of our thought. Hence as our mind dwells on holy things, we become holy.

The way of union. One way of reaching the superconscious state is by meditating on the heart of an effulgent being. St.

Francis of Assisi, as the result of his constant meditation on Christ, is said to have received the marks of the stigmata. There are hundreds of such examples in India, where the disciple, by meditating on the Master who has become one with God, also becomes one with God. From this has come the idea of liberation from all sin and sorrow by holding the thought upon a holy character—a Saviour.

Transforming power of thought. So strong is this power of thought to change the character that Sri Krishna declares in the Bhagavad-Gita: "Even if the most wicked worships Me with undivided devotion, he should be regarded as good, for he is rightly resolved. Very soon he becomes a righteous soul and attains to eternal peace."

Thought a magnet. As with good, so with evil. If evil enters our mind, it is because we have attracted it by our thought. Whenever we think of evil, we unite ourselves with it. The mind is always concentrated on something. It is constantly active and so is the body. If, therefore, we wish to preserve our welfare, we must be careful upon what we fix our thought.

Worship the Lord! The saint is always watchful. He does not let his mind run away. He never lets go of it or allows it to be disturbed by any condition of life. As a loving wife keeps her thought fixed on her absent husband and thus unites herself with him, so we should keep our thoughts fixed on the Lord, for thus we become one with Him.

Staunchness of feeling. We must have sincerity of purpose, and not merely seek a comfortable road to Truth. We must strive to cultivate staunchness of feeling and an ardent, devoted spirit.

Absorption in the Ideal. Devotion gives us steadfastness. If we are interested in one thing today, another tomorrow, we shall never attain concentration. First we must choose an Ideal. Then we must think of it, become absorbed in it, and finally lose ourselves in it. There must be nothing in our mind except our Ideal.

Devotion is concentration. Pure devotion for the one Ideal—that is concentration. When the mind through such devotion is properly collected, its power becomes tremendous and it carries us quickly to the realization of Truth.

A natural sequence. Real devotion to our Ideal will come when we have attained a certain amount of perception. We begin by paying attention to external forms of worship. Next we make the mind introspective; then concentration and meditation naturally follow. In *Samadhi,* the state of perfect peace and bliss, the body is controlled by the mind and the mind is controlled by the Self. We are part of the universal Consciousness and as we learn more and more to open ourselves to Its light, we gain greater and greater illumination.

The inner brightness. This light of the Spirit is inherent in all men. Sometimes our mind, clouded with worry and anxiety, may hide the inner brightness, but in spite of all vicissitudes, this divine, unfailing spark ever comes to our rescue with its radiant glow. We can, however, hasten its advent by responding to the divine call.

Omnipotent Soul. The Soul is omnipotent. It may remain under a cloud for a time, but in the end it cannot fail to reach the highest state of spiritual effulgence.

V.
AIDS TO MEDITATION

The superior man is watchful over himself when he is alone. —*Confucius.*

He who reigns within himself and rules passions, desires and fears is more than king. —*Milton.*

Whatsoever things are true, whatsoever things are honest, whatsoever things are just, whatsoever things are pure, whatsoever things are lovely, whatsoever things are of good report, think on these things. —*St. Paul.*

The tree which filleth the arms grew from the tiniest sprout; the tower of nine storeys rose from a little mound of earth, the journey of a thousand miles began with a single step. —*Lao-Tzu.*

BEFORE we can take up any spiritual practice, the mind must become well established in the fundamental ethical principles, such as non-injuring, non-stealing, truthfulness, continence, external and internal purity, contentment, control of the senses, study of the Scriptures and self-surrender. This means that we must not give way to jealousy, anger, hatred or unkindness by thought, word or action; we must not covet or envy; we must speak the truth fearlessly; we must observe chastity, inner and outer cleanliness and self-restraint; and we must be faithful in our higher study and in devotion to our Ideal. Until these principles are firmly fixed in the heart, no amount of outer practice can help us.

Our spiritual structure. The foundation must be right before we can construct a solid building, and the building of our character or spiritual structure can never be solid until we are well grounded in these moral qualities. They are also essential to tranquility of mind, for unless we can look within and find ourselves above reproach, we never can enjoy peace or serenity.

Injunction of Christ. Christ said, "Therefore if thou bring thy gift to the altar, and there rememberest that thy brother hath aught against thee, leave there thy gift before the altar, and go thy way. First be reconciled to thy brother, then come and offer thy gift."

When meditation is futile. If we have anything in our life that is not in accord with spiritual principles, no amount of sitting still and trying to meditate will bring us the blessing of contemplation.

Asana or posture. The next step is the practice of posture (*Asana*). One must learn to sit properly. You may ask: "What has that to do with our spiritual progress?" We imagine that we can sit in any way we wish, but that is not true.

The idea of posture. We must learn to sit in a manner which causes us to be as little conscious as possible of our physical existence; thus our mind will not be dragged down by the weight of the body and can more easily grow calm. One who has not proper control over his body is unable to make proper use of his mind: he can never concentrate—much less can he meditate. Also if the mind is not balanced, we cannot sit still, even for a few seconds. The idea of posture, therefore, is to acquire firmness of both mind and body. A man who lacks mastery over either his physical or mental organism cannot possibly gain spiritual consciousness.

Restlessness and lethargy. At first we may have to force the body to be still. We do this by making up our mind that for a stated time we will hold our body in a certain position with balance and stability. By doing this from day to day we overcome lethargy as well as physical restlessness.

Yielding to the body. How often we feel overpowered by lethargy! The body does not want to do a thing and at once we yield. Perhaps it does not feel well and so we sacrifice our spiritual practice. This means that the body is proving its supremacy over the mind, which should never be. The practice of posture, however, will help us to overcome all this, so that we shall grow less conscious of our physical and more conscious of our spiritual nature.

Correct posture. The chief suggestion in regard to posture is that the spinal column should be held in an easy, erect position, for we find that most of the conditions of ill-health arise from disorders in the spine. The position of the spine has much to do with the breath and with the flow of life-force. Unless the spine is in a proper position, neither the breathing nor the circulation of the nerve currents can be normal.

Posture frees the mind. Those who are not used to sitting straight may, in the beginning, find this practice difficult; but after a little effort, it will become easy and natural and then the mind will have greater freedom to think and to aspire.

Steadiness essential. So long as the body keeps moving, we cannot focus and elevate our thoughts. We know that a telescope needs to be steady before we can focus the lens and observe the stars or planets. Similarly these instruments of body and mind must be steady before we can focus the thought and have clear inner vision.

Balance of mind and body. Posture means a steadfast feeling—no wavering anywhere. Our body is well established, our mind is well established, neither disturbs our balance and thus we acquire a state of perfect equilibrium.

Breath. Breath is the next thing to be considered. "What can breath have to do with our spiritual development?" again you may ask.

Breath is life. Breath is life. It is the medium through which the life-current (*Prana*) flows into us, permeating our whole being and sustaining us. When a person has lost the power to breathe, we know that he has ceased to live, then we give up all hope and we say of him, "He has breathed his last."

How we should breathe. We all breathe but we do not all derive the proper benefit from our breathing. This is because we do not know how to regulate our breath. We breathe automatically, involuntarily, unconsciously; we must learn to breathe consciously, properly and rhythmically.

Pranayama or breath-control. Controlling the life-force by conscious control of the breath is known as *Pranayama*. When we understand how to do this, we can fill ourselves with *Prana*—vital energy—and thus eliminate all our impurities.

Mind controls breath. Now breath is controlled by thought. If we observe, we shall see that whenever the mind is disturbed or restless, our breathing becomes irregular, and we lose our rhythm. As a result, everything is thrown out of balance; we can no longer co-ordinate, and there is an impairment of both our physical and mental health.

Breath can be like a musical rhythm. When the body grows ill it again causes the breath to be disordered. To avoid this vicious circle, the Yogis tell us to cultivate the habit of rhythmic breathing. Not only will it enable us to store up the vital energy we already have within us, thus preventing illness, but through breath alone we can bring about such rhythm within the body that health will be restored. When our inhaling and exhaling become even, it affects us just like a musical rhythm, creating harmony throughout our entire system.

Mind must be introspective. Following these preparatory steps, our next step is to make the mind introspective. It is all very well to have some one tell us to look within, for only there shall we realize the Truth; but how to go within? We cannot do it suddenly because of the hold the body has over us. Our mind also is divided and claimed by many things. To detach ourselves from our bodily conditions and make our mind one-pointed require steady effort. Sometimes, indeed, the task seems so hard that we grow discouraged and want to give up. Those are the very moments, however, when we must hold firm. Sri Krishna, the Lord, says in the Bhagavad-Gita: Do not permit yourself to be depressed! This mind which seems so unyielding and difficult to subdue, can be subdued through constant practice of dispassion and through discrimination, O Arjuna!

Singleness of purpose. Intensity of purpose is what brings concentration and true devotion brings intensity. When we really yearn for spiritual things, our mind naturally becomes single and we surmount every difficulty. Singleness is what we want.

Penetrative thought. In order to put a thread through the eye of a needle, we have to twist the thread to a single point; if we do not, it is a difficult task to accomplish.

Similarly, the mind which has become divided through its varied interests must be made single before it can penetrate into the depth of our being. This does not mean necessarily cutting ourselves off from other interests. Singleness means that we are able to put our whole force into whatever we undertake.

The ideal of Yoga. The ideal of Yoga—of all religion and philosophy—is to make the mind single, the heart single, the purpose single. In this singleness lies the whole secret of realization. Every sage and seer has recognized this. Did not Christ say, "If therefore thine eye be single, thy whole body shall be full of light?"

Freedom of the soul. The main object of these spiritual practices is to free the soul. Freedom means completeness, no lack anywhere—no lack of knowledge, no lack of power, no lack of anything. Before we can realize this freedom, however, we must go through certain training so that past impressions may be entirely wiped out.

Why we fail to gain vision.. Many people do not gain spiritual vision because they have not paid proper attention to the preliminary stages. When we are well established in our first practices, then the greater things will come naturally. Higher study deals not only with the spiritual nature, it deals also with our human nature. We must gain mastery over the whole of our being.

Lack of collectiveness. Often people fail to realize a desired end because of lack of collectiveness in body and mind. Patanjali tells us that we must protect ourselves from the outset. Before undertaking the practice of meditation we must have so collected and stored our forces that we shall not be wanting in either physical or mental strength. If we neglect to make the foundation strong, the superstructure cannot be satisfactory.

Our first requirement. The very first requirement is to choose our inner Ideal. One cannot go contrary to one's natural spiritual instinct, therefore this instinct must guide us in our choice. Having chosen our Ideal, we must follow it in spite of failures, in spite of all obstructions. Day by day, we must hold it before us, and if we forget it, we must bring our mind back to it. In this way, the mind grows unwavering and one-pointed and meditation becomes possible.

When the soul awakes. No one else can give us an adequate idea of what meditation is, of the value or the ecstasy of it; we never can know till we ourselves taste it. Then only does the soul become wakeful, become itself, enter fully into its own element.

Conquering the unconquerable. We must, however, do everything gradually. We must not put too much pressure either on our body or our mind. This is one of the great things we have to bear in thought. We should never be impatient and overdo, but go forward steadily, accomplishing each day a little more according to our capacity. If we persist, soon we find that things which seemed impossible to conquer, have been conquered.

No need for haste. This life is not a matter of a few seconds. It did not spring just from this little beginning. It has had a past and it will have a future, so there is no need for undue hurry. If we have imperfections, we can overcome them; whatever virtues we possess, we did something to earn them and we can earn more. Understanding this, we should strive to take up these practices and carry them on with perserverance and an undepressed heart; thus gradually we shall overcome all obstacles.

Flashes of light. One little glimpse of higher things, one little proof will strengthen our faith on our journey. First we hear about a thing; then we reflect; and after thinking and reflecting, a flash of light comes to prove to us that what we heard is true. Just one little flash is enough to give us confidence to go on; then comes another and yet another, until at last the whole Truth shines. It does not happen all at once. One day we feel a sense of great serenity, of illumination, then it disappears, only to return and remain a little longer. Again it leaves us, but if we persevere, if we are not discouraged, it is sure to come back and be more abiding. To make it a permanent factor in our lives we must practise steadily.

Habit of faithful practice.

Let us form the habit of faithful practice. We cannot gain any vital end without supreme effort. This supreme effort we must make within ourselves, and we must persevere until the meditative life has become perfectly natural to us, as natural as the outer life is to us now.

Spiritual pole-star. Instead of dwelling on petty things and devoting our energy to small personal aims, we must hold our mind on larger ends. As we release it from the bondage of selfish concerns and fix it on noble, worshipful thoughts, we shall find that it will become more and more independent and free. At first it may feel a stranger in the spiritual realm; but soon it will begin to feel at home there. Then no matter how it may be engaged, always like the needle of a compass it will keep itself pointed towards the Ideal.

We must consecrate ourselves In the Infinite, the Unchanging alone we shall find a firm basis for our meditation. But to enter into relationship with That, we must consecrate ourselves. We must seek and pray and yearn for It. We must have firmness of determination and never stop until our mind gains direct contact with the all-effulgent Spirit. It is in this spiritual union that the soul attains its highest illumination.

Let us seek the inward path. Let us, therefore, go within and more within, and seek That which is our only safeguard—the divine Principle—finding which, we shall know no lack. We do not have to seek far or long before we find It. It is like a brilliant light; It is like a fragrant flower, and though we may have covered It over with non-essential thoughts and feelings, we have the power to uncover It, to make It our own.

VI.

SUPERCONSCIOUS VISION

They have sung of Him as infinite and unattainable: but I in my meditations have seen Him without sight.

—*Kabir.*

Quoth Brother Giles to a certain brother: "Father, gladly would I know what is contemplation." And that brother replied: "Father, I do not yet know." Then said Brother Giles: "Meseemeth that the grade of contemplation is a heavenly fire and a sweet devotion of the Holy Spirit, and a rapture and uplifting of the mind intoxicated in the contemplation of the unspeakable savor of the divine sweetness, and a happy, peaceful and sweet delight of soul, that is rapt and uplifted in great marvel at the glorious things of heaven above; and a burning sense within of that celestial glory unspeakable." —*Little Flowers of St. Francis.*

Make then thyself to grow to the same stature as the Greatness which transcends all measure. Leap forth from everybody; transcend all time; become Eternity.

—*Hermes Trismegistus.*

SUPERCONSCIOUS vision is one of the great dreams of all mystics, devotees and seekers. What does it mean? That our normal becomes abnormal? Some people imagine that this is the meaning. The whole idea to the average person seems very indefinite, abstract and alien to practical everyday living. But is it impractical?

Two kinds of ambition.

What is the basis of life? Can one succeed merely by clinging to the point of view of physical existence? One of the accusations made by the worldly-minded against those who take up the contemplative life is that they lack energy and ambition. Ambition for what? Wealth? Possessions? Name, fame and power? Can there not be another kind of ambition—a yearning for something more lasting, something that will shed light not only on our path but on the path of our fellow-men?

Questions close to the heart.

The thing is—do we want to walk in the darkness alone or offer up all our aspirations and faculties to God and walk in His light? Do we want to follow the impulses of our body or gather up our forces and let the higher Principle within govern us? These are questions very close to every human heart and the answers to them come from within, only from within.

The cosmic surge.

The contemplative life does not mean that we go apart and lose all practical usefulness, or that we cease to contribute our share toward the good of humanity. On the contrary, all our sympathies are quickened, our perceptions grow keener, our feelings deepen and we perform our duties with greater efficiency. We pray and meditate in order that we may have greater power, greater ability, greater clearness of vision, so that whatever we contribute will be the gift of God. We do not lose our present consciousness: it becomes enlarged. We do not lose our feelings of sympathy or love: we have a more abundant supply. Instead of centering our consciousness in our little being or in one little group, we begin to feel the pulse of the universe. The Heart of the universe takes possession of our heart and the great cosmic Life begins to surge through our life. This is the mark of genius everywhere.

The vision of the poets. John Masefield, Poet Laureate of England, expresses it with poetic fervor: "They (Homer, Aeschylus, Dante, Shakespeare) had access to an illumination which came within their beings, as sunlight comes within the sea.

All may know illumination. "I believe that this illumination exists eternally, and that all may know it in some measure by effort or through grace. Those who deny it can never have felt it. It is so intense that, compared with it, no other sensation seems to exist or to be real. It is so bright that all else seems to be shadow. It is so penetrating that in it the littlest thing, the grain of sand, the flower of the weed, or the plume upon a moth's wing, are evidences of the depth and beauty and unity of life."

Merged in the Glory. When a man attains this higher state of consciousness, it does not mean death to his mortal being.

He does not lose his identity: the lesser light is swallowed in a larger Light. It still exists, but it is merged in the greater glory. Buddha did not lose anything when he attained Nirvana. He dropped the limiting, finite self and he became the Awakened One.

This is the law.

As long as we are guided by self-will and are swept by ordinary impulses, we never find happiness or rest. It is the contemplative man who is full of joy and peace. He is not carried away by his lower instincts. He exercises perfect control over all his faculties and powers, and he gains this control through meditation. Always according to where we place our thought do we gain the result. This is the law.

Mind can be treacherous.

Constantly we are moulding our character and destiny by the thoughts we are thinking. We are free to avoid all evil, unclean, detrimental thoughts if we wish; but more often we do not wish;

we do not even make any exertion. One who provokes or injures us will rise in our mind more often than one who has given us spiritual inspiration. The mind can be in this way very treacherous.

Wrong training. Yet it is not the fault of the mind. It is the fault of the training we give to it. The mind has the power of retention; when we train it to retain only that which is helpful to us and to discard that which is harmful, then it becomes our true friend and we advance quickly.

Mind colored by contacts. Mind also has the power of absorption. Whatever we allow our mind to associate with, we absorb the quality of that. If we associate with a person who is dull, heavy, ignorant, lethargic, very soon we also begin to feel heavy and dull. Likewise when we come in contact with one who is inspiring, radiant and spiritual, those same qualities rise up in us.

Right instinct. There is a right instinct in us all which tells us what to do and what to avoid. By intelligent reasoning and discrimination every one can know the correct path to follow; but very few of us have the strength, stability, and determination to keep to that path. Why is this? Because the mind is filled with many wrong impressions which distort its true vision.

A teaching of Vedanta. According to the teaching of Vedanta, there is no need for any one to be despondent, believing that it is too late for him to begin or that he is unfitted for spiritual striving. It matters not how unfitted we may appear to be, always we can overcome.

Mind is one. We do not need a different kind of mind to attain higher consciousness. It is the same mind which creates bondage for us and which liberates us. It is the same mind which makes us happy or miserable. The difference lies wholly in the training it has received.

No set rules for meditation. There are no set rules for meditation, as there are no set rules for spiritual evolution in any form. Various suggestions are offered us by the great philosophies and religions of the world and we must absorb them according to our capacity. From beginning to end, the path of meditation teaches us that it is not the letter which saves us; it is the Spirit within.

The guiding hand of God. Meditation is for the thoughtful and the vigilant. No priest or minister, no gospel or form of religion, can open the door for us to that unbounded Source of blessing, nor can it be opened through material means. We ourselves must make the effort, but we need the hand of God to lead us. Without His guidance our steps will be faltering, our will frail, and our mind full of error. If, however, we turn our thoughts unfailingly toward the Divine, our nature gradually becomes transformed.

Meditation upon God. "How may we meditate on God?" you ask. God is our Father and Mother. He is the One from Whom we have descended—surely there cannot be a closer bond! Why then should we hesitate to go directly to Him? The great Saviours and saints tell us that if we would enter His kingdom we must be born again.

Mother and child. As the little child goes to its mother, in the same way we must be willing to go to the great Divine Mother and lay all our troubles at Her feet. It is the grown-up, calculating person who has endless distractions and miseries. But the selfless, childlike soul always has a feeling of serenity and the meditative sense. Such a man does nothing with self-consciousness. He does not even write a sentence thinking that he is doing it. We say, "Thy will be done;" but when it comes to actual practice, we use our own will. There is no contradiction in the life of the superconscious man.

God's world and man's world. We must not imagine that our spiritual life and our life in the world cannot blend in harmony. If they do not, there is something wrong in us. It means that our inner and outer life are not coinciding, that we are hypocrites. We think one thing and do another. When the inner and the outer blend, when our thoughts and our acts are the reproduction of one and the same ideal, then we know that we are living in accord with the Highest.

Man's divided consciousness. God has not created man with two hearts. He has not given him a divided mind. It is we who divide ourselves through our complex desires, our self-will and ambition. So long as we are possessed by these, our vision will be clouded. Superconsciousness means clarified vision, free from error and inclusive. Those who possess it grow more tolerant, more loving and enduring. One with small outlook sees only from a single angle and easily grows irritable and angry; but when the heart has become part of the universal Heart, it is never impatient or unloving.

What revives and redeems? If we feel that our life is full of darkness and despondency, barren and burdensome, it is because we have not brought the divine Light into it. Why not bring in that Light? It alone has the power to revive and redeem us.

Light of all lights. "That stainless, indivisible Brahman, pure Light of all lights, dwells in the innermost golden sheath—the core of the heart." Thus the knowers of Truth find Him within—in the depth of being.

By His Light all is lighted. "The sun does not shine there, nor the moon, nor the stars, nor do these lightnings shine there, much less this fire." The Upanishads tell man that even the sun and moon cannot reveal That. All this glamour and glory of material life, they are nothing. "When He shines, everything shines after Him; by His Light all is lighted."

The banishing of darkness.

What a wonderful lesson for us to learn! No matter how glorious we may become or how much power may be bestowed on us, let us never forget that all our strength and our blessings are dependent on that One. Even the sun draws its light from Him, and for us to feel that we are part of that Infinitude, to rely on it, to fasten our heart upon it, is the highest wisdom, the only way of salvation, the banishing of darkness from this world of misery.

VII.
THE GROUNDWORK OF THOUGHT

All that we are is the result of what we have thought, it is founded on our thought, it is made up of our thought.

—*Dhammapada.*

Tell me what that is upon which you most frequently and intensely think, that to which in your silent hours your soul most naturally turns, and I will tell you to what place of pain or peace you are travelling. —*James Allen.*

To overcome sorrow and win happiness men wander in vain, for they have not sanctified their thought, the mysterious essence of holiness. . . . What need is there of any vows save the vow to guard the thought? —*Santi-Deva.*

MAN consists primarily of his thought. Never can he achieve anything finer, greater, or more potent than his thought permits him to conceive within his soul.

Creative power of our thought.

Thoughts are more creative than action. You may laugh at this; you may say: "What are you talking about? It is action which is productive—the busy hands and feet. If we should merely sit down and think about the things we are going to do, they would never get done."

Thought inspires action. It is not that we should think, and do nothing. For the man who is thoughtful that would be impossible. People who truly think are incapable of sitting idle. Their bodies become charged with great and lofty ideas and their whole being pulsates with desire for expression.

Mind and deed must be one. We cannot play this game of life by thinking one thing and doing another. A man may pretend to be happy, but if his thoughts are unhappy, he will not pretend long. Our whole strength depends on the co-ordination of thought and action. Only through co-ordinated thoughts do we become conscious of the strength before us, behind us and all about us. Therefore, let a man think. What can he think? Not anything other than what he is.

Art of thinking. People who have learned the art of thinking or, as it is stated philosophically, who have learned to meditate, cannot be turned aside. They are carried on by the momentum of their thought.

Can exaltation endure? There are moments when everyone feels exalted and there comes a tremendous surging of power. The problem is how to make this lasting. Why is it that we cannot continue to feel this exaltation? I think we can, and there is nothing which will aid us more than the cultivation of this art.

Meditative mind and meditation. Projected thought, continuous thought, subtle and potent thought—thought which cannot be broken—that is my definition of meditation, and the mind which is so firmly set upon a subject, a theme or an ideal that it can find its way through obscure and difficult avenues without being defeated is the meditative mind.

Character and the machine. Today we are inclined to depend on machinery. It is the age for manufacture. Science is widening out in many directions. Sometimes it seems as if it were on the point of being able to create, but I feel sure that it will never produce any machine or device that will be able to create thought. It may be able to evolve something in the way of diabolical machines by which we can destroy one another, or machines which can substitute mental action up to a certain point, but never can it bring about that subtlest of creations—the creation of character—the fine thought, the idealistic conception, the practical wisdom which we find in Christ, in Buddha, in St. Francis, and in the lives of all sages of every country and age. These qualities can be evolved only by man, as his thought and aspiration enable him to come in close alliance with his Maker.

God and the robot. —Sir Arthur Eddington, world-famous English astronomer, in a recent interview gives his views in regard to the concept of God and a mechanical universe.

Referring especially to the robot—that marvelous creation of modern science, which can walk, talk, labor, even think—he says:

The inescapable test.

"I say to the creator of the robot, 'You have shown us a mechanical creature which thinks. But remember the inescapable test—is it concerned with truth as I am? Then will I acknowledge that it is indeed myself.' We must have a creature to whom it matters, in any non-utilitarian sense, what it thinks and believes.

What does it all mean?

"We behold these innumerable suns rolling on—trees, flowers, oceans that heave in storms. What does it all mean? We cannot answer in terms of leaping electrons or mathematical equations. So when we seek the meaning in consciousness, we find that it is about a Spirit, within which truth has its shrine. These stirrings of consciousness are greater than our individual personalities. Religion presents this side of experience as a matter of everyday life. We have to grasp it in the form of familiar recognition and not as a series of abstract scientific statements. If God is part of everyday life, it does no harm to think and speak of Him unscientifically, whatever the philosophic critics may say."

Explorers of the Spirit. Philosophers, wise men, mystics are explorers, not so much of the mortal realm in search of treasure as of the realm of mind in search of Truth; and what they have found, they have expressed through great thoughts, and words, and deeds.

The man of tranquil soul The man of tranquil soul, whose thought has made his mind immovable as the Northern star, expresses himself in such a way as to leave a lasting impression upon the lives of men.

Be balanced but not earth-bound. Often the worldly-wise say, "Why bother with these vague spiritual matters—keep your feet on the ground." It is good to keep one's feet on the ground, in the sense of being balanced, but it is possible to grow so heavy with thoughts of worry, care and material concerns that we become earth-bound altogether. Then we feel the weight of the world and the world feels the weight of us. That is why we have to learn to live apart from the world, at least in our hours of exaltation, so that instead of inhaling noxious odors, we may inhale a fragrant breath. In India there are Ashramas—sacred retreats—where at dawn one breathes not only the spirit of beauty but the spirit of sanctity as well.

Man's endowment. What is it that creates such an atmosphere of holiness and keeps it alive like a flaming candle? It is man. God has endowed man with power to create lovely things, to pen lovely thoughts, to be a definite factor in building things of enduring loveliness—and it is by thought that he does it. Also by thought he is able to destroy.

Creative thought. Thought is creative. Every time we think, we create, but the strength, the permanence of our creation depends on the one-pointedness, the clarity, the strength of our thought, and how continuously we hold it. Thought can be like a line drawn by a pencil, quickly to be rubbed out, or it can be fixed and enduring. It can be pure and lofty, as in the Upanishads, or it can be small and hateful. Man, in the madness of his brain, can dwell so persistently on a cruel, destructive thought, can grind it so deeply into his consciousness that finally it will result either in some crime or in a horrible disaster. He can create the most wonderful atmosphere, thus breaking his loneliness; also he can deprive himself of solitude and peace, can dwell in the midst of chaos and confusion, even while living in a mountain cave, or in a wilderness where is nothing but stillness.

The Tree of Fulfillment. According to an ancient parable, a man once was wandering through the forest when suddenly he came upon a beautiful tree, and being weary, he sat down beneath its shade. Now it happened that this was a tree which in India they call *Kalpataru,* the Tree of Fulfillment. Sitting under it, whatever a man thinks materializes at once. So, when this man said, "Oh, I am tired! I wish I could lie on something soft!" immediately he found himself upon a couch. After lying there a while in pure wonderment, he said, "I am hungry; if only I could have some food!" and hardly had he wished for it when special food was placed before him. As his fancy took hold of him, the man's desires became more and more enlarged. Everything he wished for came, even a wife; but just at the point of greatest fulfillment, suddenly he thought, "Perchance a tiger may appear!" And the tiger also came and swallowed him.

The tigers of our mental jungle.

So with us. Often we feel that we are receiving great good, when, all at once, an uncontrolled thought—a tiger in the form of wrath or envy or greed—comes and destroys everything that we have gained, unless we can quickly co ordinate and preserve ourselves by the art of meditation.

Our world the creation of mind.

The beautiful things we see in the world—cities and countries, homes and places of pilgrimage—all are the products of man's mind. Man can think of himself as a sinner, and by so thinking, can make himself an even greater sinner. He can start with the thought of failure, and by dwelling on it, enlarge it till it becomes a veritable catastrophe, or, through his mind, he can lift his head and raise his standard high, even when there is nothing outer to sustain him. He can build up something very beautiful, very vital and constructive, even though he may be standing upon ruins.

Danger of obsession. If a man is not capable of manipulating his own thought, all other things are of no value to him. Suppose you come in contact with a source of great power and do not know how to handle that power, you will be overwhelmed by it. If your mind is not balanced, it may develop into a case of obsession—into something which takes possession of your mind and becomes a malignant force in the world. Do not think that this is fancy, merely a harrowing picture I am giving you to discourage you from seeking power. Who is worthy to gain power? Only that man who has become well-governed, whose mind is obedient like a faithful servant.

Way of discipleship. People often ask about discipleship. He who would be a disciple, let him make his own mind his disciple, otherwise, though all the blessings of the world may come, he will not be able to retain them.

Inner refreshment. Find time to co-ordinate yourself and get away from all outer turmoil. We have plenty of time during the twenty-four hours of the day for our domestic duties, for our business and our worries, so surely we can take a few minutes to refresh ourselves inwardly. We need this in order that we may not feel defeated by life itself. We need it just as we need a daily bath for our physical refreshment. But the inner freshening no outer condition can give us: it comes through systematic control of thought.

No defect insurmountable. Whatever defects there may be in our life, though they may seem insurmountable, we can altogether wipe them out and start with a clean slate, by learning the art of thinking and meditating.

All-powerful mind. Knowledge is not just what we acquire through borrowing; it is something which we must make our own. We may, however, find inspiration and a great deal of help from that which comes to us from others. The thought and teaching contained in the literature of the world may stimulate us to such an extent that we ourselves shall be moved to create; but it is our own thoughts which sustain us and enable us to enter into the spiritual realm, and these we can govern. As one of the great teachers tells us: "It is the mind that makes one wise or ignorant, bound or emancipated." Everything depends upon a man's own mind.

India's basis of education.

In India the whole educational system was based on this concept. It should play a very vital part in the training of children. What avails if we give a child merely a little intellectual training, fill his mind with information and mechanical knowledge, unless at the same time we build his character, thus developing his insight into his own inherent power, so that he may learn to create and co-ordinate?

Our divine heritage. Mind is a divine heritage; it can be our safeguard, our stepping-stone toward the spiritual kingdom. To recognize this is the highest form of intelligence. The ancient leaders of men urged this recognition upon their followers and today we need it even more than they did, surrounded as we are with the glamour of material civilization. This civilization we call advancement. Let it then prove to be so.

Individual responsibility. A machine when it is guided by well-balanced intelligence can be of enormous benefit to man, but if it is controlled by a vicious instinct, it may prove destructive. Therefore, whether our science, our inventions, and our material achievements represent real progress or not, depends on what thoughts we are thinking. Thoughts of hatred will destroy all the beautiful things we see before us, even those we have created, whereas thoughts based on nobility, idealism, and the productive instinct will enhance our own happiness, and will enlarge the beauty, peace and prosperity of all; for in each individual life lies the responsibility for the good and evil of the whole.

Our mental jungle.

We have a way of saying, "This world is full of evil; we cannot trust any one." A thoughtful man, however, sees that he has a very large share in that evil, and even though he may be thrust into the midst of calamity, he will overcome it through his mental strength. There are people who can tame tigers and venomous snakes. Same way, man, through his thought, can make the lower instincts become aware that he is the supreme master.

The key which unlocks.

"The key to every man is his own thought," says Emerson. The man who desires to become a master-criminal naturally unfolds that type of thought. Yet it is in his own power to unlock the doors of his immortal nature and set himself free.

Slaves to our instincts. If this is even halfway true, is it not strange that we should allow ourselves to be dragged hither and thither by our unruly instincts and desires, by our suspicion, despondency and doubt?

An ancient commentary. The "Maharamayana," an ancient Hindu Scripture, comments: "Know this as a transcendent truth, and capable of preventing all your future transmigrations in this world, that you should become accustomed to the free agency of all your actions without being dragged to them by your desires."

Kingdom of God a treasure-house. Perfect control of the mind is not easy. Kingdom of God is a treasure-house fortified by impregnable walls—and it can be entered by no other means than the life within. Life within is so subtle, it can penetrate everything. Kingdom of God is for those alone who have learned the right use of thought and the use of right thought. Therein lies the secret. When we think right, nothing can go wrong. Write this in your mind.

Realization comes from within. In this life of ours, others may help us, may support us for a moment when we are fallen, may seek to awaken us to our own true nature, but realization must come from within.

Success comes with trying. If our feet are faltering and we cannot hold ourselves erect, then let us do as much as we are capable of doing; gradually we shall be able to do more.

The guiding Power. There is a Power that guides our steps, and as we relate ourselves to That through our thoughts and through the feelings that are born of our thoughts, we learn to stand upon the Rock of Truth. Then whatever happens in the outer world, we remain unshaken and unshakable.

VIII.
PRACTICAL HINTS
FIXITY OF PURPOSE

THOSE who fixing their minds on Me worship Me with perpetual devotion, endowed with supreme faith, to my mind they are the best knowers of Yoga.

—*Bhagavad-Gita.*

So go ahead, my children, and never lose sight of your Ideal! Go onward and never stop until you have reached the Goal. Reaching a particular stage, do not run away with the idea that you have come to your journey's end. Work is only the first stage of the journey. Bear in mind that doing things *unattached* is exceedingly difficult; that therefore the path of love is better suited to this age, and that work, even if unattached, is not the end of your life, but only a means to the end. So march on, and never halt till you have come up to the great Ideal of your life—*the seeing of God.* —*Sri Ramakrishna.*

In studying the wisdom of the sages it is imperative to have one definite aim—that of becoming a true man. The ancients said that he who could will could always accomplish, and that determination was half the battle. Once we have a definite aim, we become as bowmen with arrows trained on the target, or as travellers already moving toward their destination. In formulating our aims, let us be courageous rather than timid, and seek the truth even as the hungry man seeks food, the thirsty water, allowing nothing to hinder us as we press on toward the goal. Chu said: "Unless the aim be single, it cannot succeed." Then let him who ventures in the quest for true wisdom be single-minded, with the concentration of a setting hen or of a cat watching her prey. —*Kaibara Ekken.*

If a man's faith is unsteady, if he does not know the true law, if his peace of mind is troubled, his knowledge will never be perfect. Wise people, meditative, steady, . . . attain to Nirvana, the highest happiness.

—*Gautama Buddha.*

Shake off your sleep, and seek the grace of the Lord with steadfast devotion. Make the mind one-pointed like the mariner's compass. In whatever direction the ship may sail, the compass always points to the north, thus keeping the ship on its course. Even so with the human mind. If it is fixed on God, there will be nothing to fear. If by chance one is thrown into a bad environment, even then his faith and devotion will remain unshaken. The moment he hears any talk about God, he will become mad with divine love—just as the flint, lying under water for a hundred years, when taken out and struck, emits sparks.

—*Swami Brahmananda.*

THOUGHT

As a fire without fuel dies down on the hearth, thus do the thoughts, when all activity ceases, become quiet in their place.

For thoughts alone cause the round of births. Let a man strive to purify his thoughts. What a man thinks, that he is: this is the old secret.

By the serenity of his thoughts a man blots out all actions, whether good or bad. Dwelling within his Self with serene thoughts, he obtains imperishable happiness.

If the thoughts of a man were so fixed on *Brahman* (the Supreme) as they are on the things of this world, who would not then be freed from bondage!

—*Maitrayana-Brahmana-Upanishad.*

Man with his passions is like the tamer of lions and bears in a menagerie. To bridle them, train them, make domestic animals, servants out of them is the business of every man.

Feeling arises independently of man's will; but thought either approves or disapproves feeling and stimulates or retards it accordingly. Hence everything depends on thought.

The seed is unseen in the ground, but from it alone the huge tree grows. A thought is just as imperceptible, but from it alone grow the greatest events in human life. All human deeds, good or bad, arise from thoughts.

We often think that our life is real only when we come in contact with people. This is untrue. Our life is most real when we are by ourselves alone, absorbed in our own thoughts. We attain to all our best actions not by impetuous outbursts but, on the contrary, by quiet inner work over our own souls. Every truth already exists in the soul of every man. Only keep from deadening it with falsehood and sooner or later it will be revealed to you. Truth, like gold, is to be obtained not by its growth, but by washing away from it all that is not gold. This liberation is accomplished by effort of thought.

—*Tolstoy.*

Thought builds the universe. . . . Anything may be achieved by thought. Death, disease, poverty, humiliation, any or all of these may be overcome. . . .

This force ought always to be used in constructive forms. We ought always to devote it to what are called positive ends. We should never use it for hatred or jealousy or anger, but always in love and faith, and for the upbuilding of something. . . .

The use of mental powers for directly destructive ends has always been regarded as accursed. It is what the West calls black magic, and certainly recoils upon the user in very terrible ways. A large beneficence should distinguish the man who knows the power of his own thought. . . .

The less selfish the thing we wish for, the

greater and keener will be the accumulated and multiplied power of our thought battery. Our thought must be clear and ordered. When this is done, we shall see, to our surprise, that it has become creative.

—*Aurobindo Ghose.*

You can control nothing but your own mind. Even your two-year-old babe may defy you by the instinctive force of its personality. But your own mind you can control. Your own mind is a sacred enclosure into which nothing harmful can enter except by your permission. Your own mind has the power to transmute every external phenomenon to its own purposes.

If happiness arises from cheerfulness, kindliness and rectitude (and who will deny it?), what possible combination of circumstances is going to make you unhappy, so long as the machine remains in order? . . .

Look within. The Kingdom of Heaven is

within you. "Oh yes," you protest, "all that's old. Epictetus said that. Christ said that." They did. I admit it readily. But if you were ruffled this morning because your motor omnibus broke down and you had to take a cab, then, so far as you are concerned, these great teachers lived in vain. . . . And all because you have a sort of notion that a saying said two thousand years ago cannot be practical. —*Arnold Bennett.*

CONCENTRATION

As a fletcher makes straight his arrow, a wise man makes straight his trembling and unsteady thought, which is difficult to guard, difficult to hold back. Let the wise man guard his thoughts. Thoughts well-guarded bring happiness. —*Gautama Buddha.*

A Yogi should constantly practise concentration of the heart, remaining in seclusion alone, subduing his body and mind and being free from longing and possession (sense of ownership). In a cleanly spot, having established his seat firmly, neither too high nor too low, with a cloth, skin and Kusha grass, placed one on the other; being seated there, making the mind one-pointed and subduing the activities of mind and senses, let him practise Yoga for self-purification. Let him hold his body, head and neck erect and motionless, fixing the gaze on the tip of his nose, not looking around. Being serene-hearted and fearless, ever steadfast in the vow of *Brahmacharya* (continence) and controlling the mind, let him sit steadfastly absorbed in thoughts of Me, regarding Me as his supreme goal. Thus ever keeping himself steadfast, the Yogi of subdued mind attains eternal peace and freedom, which abide in Me.

But, O Arjuna, (the practice of) Yoga is not for him who eats too much or who does not eat at all, nor for him who sleeps too much or keeps awake (in excess). He who is moderate in eating and recreation, moderate in his efforts in work, moderate in sleep and wakefulness, (his practice of) Yoga becomes the destroyer of all misery. When the mind, completely subdued, rests in Self alone, free from longing for all objects of desire, then he is said to be a *Yukta* (steadfast in Self-knowledge). . . .

In that state, transcending the senses, the Yogi feels that infinite bliss which is perceived by the purified understanding; knowing that and being established therein, he never falls back from his real state (of Self-knowledge); after having attained which, no other gain seems greater; being established wherein, he is not overwhelmed even by great sorrow. Know that state of separation from the contact with pain as Yoga. This Yoga should be practised with perseverance and undepressed heart.

Abandoning without reserve all the desires born of mental fancies, and restraining completely by the mind the entire group of the senses from all directions, with understanding held by firmness and mind established in the Self, let him (thus) by degrees attain tranquillity; let him not think of anything else. Wheresoever the restless and unsteady mind may wander away, let him withdraw it from there and bring it under the control of the Self alone.

He whose passions are quieted and mind perfectly tranquil, who has become one with Brahman, being freed from all impurities, to such a Yogi comes supreme bliss. Thus constantly holding the mind steadfast, the Yogi, whose sins are shaken off, easily attains the infinite bliss, born of contact with Brahman.

—*Bhagavad-Gita.*

This is the rule for achieving concentration: restraint of the breath, restraint of the senses, meditation, fixed attention, investigation, absorption, these are called the sixfold

Yoga. When beholding by this Yoga, he beholds the gold-colored Maker,—the Lord, the Person, *Brahman,* the Cause; then the sage, leaving behind good and evil, makes everything (breath, organs of sense, body, etc.) to be one in the Highest Indestructible.

—*Maitrayana-Brahmana-Upanishad.*

Nature shows us constantly that at the back of every action there should be a great repose. This holds good from the minutest growth to the most powerful tornado. It should be so with us not only in the simple, daily duties, but in all things up to the most intense activity possible to man. . . .

How can we expect repose of mind when we have not even repose of muscle? . . .

True concentration of mind means the ability to drop every subject but that centred upon. Tell a man to concentrate his mind on a difficult problem until he has worked it out—he will clench his fists, tighten his throat, hold his teeth hard together, and contract nobody knows how many more muscles in his body, burning and wasting fuel in a hundred or more places where it should be saved. This is *not* concentration. Concentration means the focusing of a force; and when the mathematical faculty of the brain alone should be at work, the force is not focused if it is at the same time flying over all other parts of the body in useless strain of innumerable muscles. —*Annie Payson Call.*

First began the stilling of mind and soul. The very activity of the brain may make a man a bad listener, and listening was our goal. The intellect needs to learn how to be still, no less than the body, if it is to concentrate all its powers. A single and sustained attention to God is the crux of the whole matter.

This preparation may take long. It is worth persisting in until it has gained its end, until mind and soul are silent unto God.

Thus we pass to the centre of our silence. The will is at its highest activity. As an insect poised in the air, seemingly motionless, with wings in such rapid motion that they are invisible, is all the while sustained by its resistance to the air, so the will in this listening is not passive. It holds fast to its rest in God by sustained resistance to all that would drag it down or invade its silence. This is far from making the mind a blank. It is the filling of the mind with God to the exclusion of all else.

Not in words, nor visions, nor signs, did we look for the communications of God. . . . Only we knew God and we knew that we knew Him. —*Quaker Practice of Silence.*

For the extremely energetic, concentration is near.

Disease, mental laziness, doubt, cessation, false perception, non-attaining concentration, and falling away from the state when obtained, are the obstructing distractions.

Grief, mental distress, tremor of the body, irregular breathing, accompany non-retention of concentration.

To remedy this, the practice of one subject should be made.

—*Patanjali Yoga Aphorisms.*

Music develops in its own elect that power of concentration on an idea, that form of Yoga, that is purely European, having the traits of action and domination that are characteristic of the West. . . . In no other musician has the embrace of thought been more violent, more continuous, more super-human (than in Beethoven). Once Beethoven takes hold upon an idea, he never lets it go until he possesses it wholly. . . .

Now I myself, when studying the essence of Beethoven's creative genius, had been struck by the "furious concentration" that is the characteristic mark of it, and that distinguishes him from all the other composers of his epoch. I had insisted on this point in my commemorative address at Vienna: "All his music bears the imprint of an extraordinary passion for unity. . . . The whole of his work is stamped with the seal of a will of iron; we feel that the man's glance is sunk in the idea with a terrific fixity. . . .

"It is a natural disposition. From infancy Beethoven is absorbed in his interior vision, that eyeless vision that is at once of the whole body and of the whole spirit. When an idea occurred to him in the crowded street, in the course of a walk or of a conversation, he had, as he used to say, a *raptus;* he no longer belonged to himself but to the idea; he never loses his hold on it until he has made it his. Nothing will distract him from the pursuit. He described this frantic chase to Bettina in the language of hallucination: 'I pursue it, I grasp it, I see it fly from me and lose itself in the seething mass. I seize it again with renewed passion, I can no longer separate myself from it; I have to multiply it in a spasm of ecstasy, in all its modulations.' "

—*Romain Rolland.*

MEDITATION

Now what most contributes to the growth of these wings (of the soul) is meditation, by which we learn little by little to wean our affections from earthly things, and to get a habit of contemplating the things that are immaterial and intelligible, and to shake off the pollutions it has contracted by its union with the terrestrial and mortal body. And, indeed, by these advantages it revives in some manner, it rouses up itself, it is filled with divine vigor and reunites itself to the Intelligent Perfection within. —*Hierocles.*

Those forms of concentration that bring extraordinary sense perceptions cause perseverance of the mind.

(By the meditation on) the Effulgent One which is beyond all sorrow;

Or (by meditation on) the heart that has given up all attachment to sense objects;

Or by meditating on the knowledge that comes in sleep;

Or by the meditation on anything that appeals to one as good—

The Yogi's mind, thus meditating, becomes unobstructed from the atomic to the Infinite.

—*Patanjali Yoga Aphorisms.*

There is, in sanest hours, a consciousness, a thought that rises, independent, lifted out from all else, calm—like the stars—shining, eternal. This is the thought of identity—yours for you, whoever you are, as mine for me. Miracle of miracles, beyond statement, most spiritual and vaguest of earth's dreams, yet hardest basic fact, and only entrance to all facts. . . .

I should say, indeed, that only in the perfect uncontamination and solitariness of individuality may the spirituality of religion positively come forth at all. Only here, and on such terms, the meditation, the devout ecstasy, the soaring flight. Only here, communion with the mysteries, the eternal problems—whence? whither?

Alone, and identity, and the mood—and the soul emerges, and all statements, churches, sermons melt away like vapors. Alone, and silent thought and awe, and aspiration—and then the interior consciousness, like a hitherto unseen inscription in magic ink, beams out its wondrous lines to the sense. Bibles may convey and priests expound, but it is exclusively for the noiseless operation of one's isolated self to enter the pure ether of veneration, reach the divine levels, and commune with the unutterable. —*Walt Whitman.*

I have never had any revelations through anaesthetics, but a kind of waking trance—

this for lack of a better word—I have frequently had, quite up from boyhood, when I have been all alone. This has come upon me through repeating my own name to myself, silently, till all at once, as it were, out of the intensity of the consciousness of individuality, individuality itself seemed to dissolve and fade away in boundless being, and this not a confused state but the clearest, the surest of the surest, utterly beyond words—when death was an almost laughable impossibility—the loss of personality (if so it were) seeming no extinction but the only true life.

—*Tennyson.*

The Bodhisattva is said to have well grasped the teachings of the Tathagatas when, all alone in a lonely place, by means of his Transcendental Intelligence, he walks the path leading to Nirvana. Thereon his mind will unfold by perceiving, thinking, meditating, and abiding in the practice of concentration, until he attains the "Turning about" at the source of habit-energy. He will thereafter lead a life of excellent deeds. His mind concentrated on the state of Buddhahood, he will become thoroughly conversant with the noble truth of self-realization; he will become perfect master of his own mind; he will be like a gem radiating many colors; he will be able to assume bodies of transformation; he will be able to enter into the minds of all to help them; and, finally, by gradually ascending the stages he will become established in the perfect Transcendental Intelligence of the Tathagatas. —*Lankavatara Sutra.*

Fixing the mind on the lotus of the heart, or on the centre of the head, is what is called *Dharana* (concentration). When remaining in one place, making one place as the base, when the waves of the mind rise up, without being touched by other waves—when all other waves have stopped—and one wave only rises in the mind, that is called *Dhyana* (meditation). When no basis is necessary, when the whole of the mind has become one wave, "one-formedness," it is called *Samadhi* (superconsciousness).

Imagine a lotus upon the top of the head, several inches up, and virtue as its centre, the stalk as knowledge. The eight petals of the lotus are the eight powers of the Yogi. Inside, the stamens and pistils are renunciation. If the Yogi refuses the external powers, he will come to salvation. So the eight petals of the lotus are the eight powers, but the internal stamens and pistils are the extreme renunciation, the renunciation of all these.

Inside of that lotus, think of the Golden One, the Almighty, the Intangible, He whose name is *Om*, the Inexpressible, surrounded with effulgent light. Meditate on that.

Think of a space in your heart, and in the midst of that space think that a flame is burning. Think of that flame as your own soul, and inside that flame is another space, effulgent, and that is the Soul of your soul, God. Meditate upon that in the heart.

Chastity, non-injuring, pardoning every one, are all different *Vrittis* (qualities of mind). Be not afraid if you are not perfect in all of these; work, and the others will come. He who has given up all attachment, all fear and all anger, he whose whole soul has gone unto the Lord, he who has taken refuge in the Lord, whose heart has become purified, with whatsoever desire he comes to the Lord He will grant that to him.

—*Swami Vivekananda.*

TRANSCENDING THOUGHT

When a man, having freed his mind from sloth, distraction and vacillation, becomes as it were delivered from his mind, that is the highest point.

The mind must be restrained in the heart

till it comes to an end;—that is knowledge; that is liberty; all the rest are extensions of the ties (which bind us to this life).

That happiness which belongs to a mind which by deep meditation has been washed clean from all impurity and has entered within the Self cannot be described by words; it can be felt by the inward power only.

Mind alone is the cause of bondage and liberty for men; if attached to the world, it becomes bound; if free from the world, that is liberty. –*Maitrayana-Brahmana-Upanishad.*

The concentration called *Right Knowledge* is that which is followed by reasoning, discrimination, bliss, unqualified ego (pure essential being).

There is another concentration which is attained by the constant practice of cessation of all mental activity, in which the mind retains only the unmanifested impressions.

—*Patanjali Yoga Aphorisms.*

And there is, further, the most Divine Knowledge of Almighty God, which is known through not knowing (*agnosia*) during the union above mind; when the mind, having stood apart from all existing things, then having dismissed also itself, has been made one with the superluminous rays, thence and there being illuminated by the unsearchable depth of wisdom.

—*Dionysius the Areopagite.*

If we would meet God above the natural world, we must enter into Him by a quickened faith; and there, in simplicity, in peace and freedom, we shall dwell, confirmed in love, in perfect nudity of spirit. When love has lifted us above objects, above light, into the holy darkness, we are transfigured by the eternal Word, like unto the Father. . . . We contemplate what we are and we are what we contemplate. . . Contemplation of the Superessential passes into communion. Yet this contemplation has a further stage when life dies and love fails. For as we enter the darkness we are seized by the single ray, which shining from the ocean of light where dwells our peace, immerses us in the Superessential. . . .

Words cannot tell it, silence has no power to hold it within its bounds; intelligence, reason, the creature itself, all are transcended. This simple possession by God is life eternal enjoyed in the fathomless abyss. It is herein, beyond reason, that we await the peace of the Divine changelessness. —*Van Ruysbroeck.*

Indian philosophy . . . is, to go to the essential point at once, incomparable with ours, already because it is not based upon the work of thought. Think of the traditional Indian method of teaching as it is referred to every now and then in the Upanishads: if a pupil puts a question, the teacher does not answer him directly, but merely says: Come and live with me for ten years. And during these ten years he does not teach him as we understand it; he merely gives him a phrase to meditate. The disciple is not meant to think about it, to analyze it, to evolve, construct something out of it—he is to sink himself, as it were, into the phrase until it has taken complete possession of his soul. . . .

According to Indian conviction, *Brahma-vidya,* the realization of being . . . is not attainable by the process of thinking. Thinking is believed to move in its original sphere, without ever leading beyond it. Just as no amount of development can lead the senses to perceive thought, so no amount of thinking could lead to metaphysical realization. This can be attained only by the man who reaches a new level of consciousness. . . . Therefore, for purposes of study, it is not a question of the work of thought, but of becoming profound in oneself: it is not a question of how to fathom reality by means of a given instrument, but of how to fashion a new and better one. . . . Man must rise above his secular instrument for recognition, . . . his consciousness must, instead of cleaving to the surface, learn to reflect the spirit of profundity which is the primary cause of his being. —*Count Hermann Keyserling.*

For at that time a man can put away all the imaginings that present themselves to him, hush the understanding, calm the memory, and fix it upon our Lord, considering how he is in His presence, making now no speculations upon the secret things of God.

Let a man imprison himself within his own self, in the centre of his soul, wherein is the image of God, and there let him wait upon Him, as one listens to another speaking from some high tower, or as though he had Him within his heart and as if in all creation there were no other thing save God and his soul.

Even himself should he forget, and that which he is doing, for, as one of the Fathers said, "That prayer is perfect in which he who is praying remembers not that he is praying."

Some few there are so far captivated by the love of God, that hardly have they begun to think upon Him when immediately the memory of His dear Name melts all their being. . . . And others, not only in the exercise of prayer, but apart from it, are so absorbed and immersed in God that they forget all things—yea, even themselves—for Him.

—*Piedro de Alcantara.*

There comes a time, however, and at last, when . . . the brain ceases from its terrified and insatiate quest. . . . The man at last lets Thought go; he glides below it into the quiet feeling, the quiet sense of his own identity with the Self of other things—of the universe. He glides past the feeling into the very identity itself. . . . He leans back in silence on that inner being, and bars off for a time every thought, every movement of the mind, every impulse to action, or whatever in the faintest degree may stand between him and That; and so there comes to him a sense of absolute repose, a consciousness of immense and universal power. . . . This is the Divine Yoga or Union, from which really all life, all Creation, proceeds. —*Edward Carpenter.*

Sri Ramakrishna Deva passed into the ineffable Glory. Before that rapturous ecstasy, the senses and mind stopped their functions. The universe rolled away from his vision—even space itself melted away. The soul lost itself in the Self, and all idea of duality, of subject and object was effaced. The limitations were gone and finite space was one with infinite space. Beyond speech, beyond experience and beyond thought, Sri Ramakrishna had realized the Absolute.

—*Life of Sri Ramakrishna.*